Swing Hard in Case You Hit It

A Brief Guide for the Novice Golfer

Second Edition

By

Tom Stevens

Swing Hard in Case You Hit It

Copyright © Tom Stevens ISBN: 9798407697091

All rights reserved. No part of this book maybe reproduced or transmitted in any form or by any means, electronic or mechanical including photocopying, recording, or by any information storage and retrieval system without permission in writing from the copyright owner.

Tom Stevens

Swing Hard in Case You Hit It

The views expressed in this work are solely those of the author and do not necessarily reflect the views of the publisher, and the publisher herby disclaim any responsibility for them.

Tom Stevens

DEDICATION

To my dad for introducing me to the game, and my mom as my junior tournament "chauffeur," as well to current and past playing partners and teaching professionals, as follows (in alphabetical order):

Players

Greg Beale

John Briski

The Burns family (Bob, Joanne, Janet and David)

Ian Crebbin

Bill "Dunk" Dunkerley

Justin "The Hawk" Hogan (no relation to Ben Hogan)

Will Hicks

Ed Jackson

John Lam

Michael Lee

Tom Stevens

Swing Hard in Case You Hit It

Charles Madison

Bill Milne

Raymond Oh

Grant Oh

Craig Sands

Tom Streng

Paul Webber

Joel Wifler

Neil Yack

Teaching Professionals

Doug Curls (Florida Club Fitter)

Leon Decaire (Canadian PGA Teaching Pro)

John Hayes (Florida PGA Teaching Pro)

Dave Pederson (Florida PGA Teaching Pro)

Pat Owen (United States Naval Academy Head Coach)

Tom Stevens

Swing Hard in Case You Hit It

Bill Richardson (Canadian PGA Teaching Pro)

Casey Steed (Florida PGA Teaching Pro)

Dennis Winters (Mid-Atlantic PGA Teaching Pro)

PGA Tour Professionals

Ben Hogan

Justin Leonard

Phil Mickelson

Jack Nicklaus

Lee Trevino

Jim Thorpe

Calvin Peete

Gary Player

Tom Watson

Television Broadcasters

Tom Stevens

Swing Hard in Case You Hit It

David Feherty

Vern Lundquist

Bill Macatee

Gary McCord

Jim Nantz

Pat Summerall

Ken Venturi

Media and Podcast Channels

The Gary and Dino Show Podcast

Chris and Stacy Woods

Swing Hard in Case You Hit It

This page has been intentionally left blank.

Tom Stevens

Swing Hard in Case You Hit It

Table of Contents

Introduction	10
Popularity of Golf	12
Wardrobe and Equipment	15
Health	37
Socializing	44
The Game Itself	52
Putting All Together	67
Conclusion	72

Tom Stevens

INTRODUCTION

This book is for novice golfers; it is a brief information to the various aspects of the game from an amateur's point of view.

Now a fair question is, "why should I read your book?" Well, because there isn't a book for the novice golfer that contains a brief introduction to most aspects of the game. After all, no current tour player will sit down and write a book like this--they're busy playing cashing in on endorsement money.

Having never played on any tour (at least not yet) nor being a PGA certified teaching professional, my passion for the game remains active, and it has been for the past 40 years.

Born to American parents in Toronto, Ontario, Canada, I played high school golf for two years at Eastern H.S. of Commerce in Toronto (same school as comedian/actor Jim Carrey). Joined the US Air Force (1985- 1989). Graduated with a degree in Electrical Engineering from Capitol College, now Capitol Technology University, in 1998.

I started playing golf in the spring of 1978; it took me four years to break 80 i.e., 78. Additionally, I also caddied for a local golf professional for a while and attempted to qualify for the 1994 US Public Links

Championship. Can't begin to count how many over pars that involved, yeesh!

I have attended 10 US Open sectional qualifiers, three LPGA championships, one US Senior Open, four Canadian Opens, two Web.com tournaments, twelve NCAA tournaments (at the US Naval Academy); and many PGA tour tournaments.

I admit my golfing resume *is slim to none*, but my passion for the game is of major championship quality, if I do say so myself. Currently, I play to a handicap of 8.1.

POPULARITY OF GOLF

Golf is a great game that tests your emotions—anger, patience, fear, anxiety, and tranquility—and this holds true for beginners to tour professionals, particularly when playing any of the major golf championships, such as the United States Golf Association's (USGA) Men's Open. The late USGA President, Sandy Tatum had stated back in 1974, when U.S. Open players were complaining of the level of course difficulty, (paraphrasing), *"...that we're not here to embarrass the pros, we're here to recognize them..."* [1]

Needless to say, Mr. Tatum's statement became the tournament mantra for the national championship. However, in your case, this game is largely, at this point, just a hobby. Speaking from experience, the game will over time capture not only your curiosity but perhaps become an obsession (and it will...). Be that as it may, there will be times you'll wish you'd never played this game; trust me, we've all gone through it, or will do at some point. All golfers have felt and displayed various types of derision toward the game, so you're not alone. On the flipside it's a game you can play at any age.

I don't know who coined the phrasing or maybe I discovered it, but golf is equivalent to an addictive

---

[1] http://www.golf.com/tour-news/2017/06/23/remembering-sandy-tatum-golf-ambassador-who-deeply-loved-game

narcotic such that *it's the one great shot that keeps you coming back!*

Note: I'll be using the phrase "corporate" throughout this book. The reason for my phrasing is that from my experience in the corporate world, I've asked playing partners at what age did they pick up the game, and their responses have been around 24-years-old (in this case, the mid-1990s). I notice the game's steady popularity in the early 1990's. Then the game sored exponentially when Tiger Woods won his first Masters Tournament in 1997.

Most, if not all, golf development starts during the early teenage years (I started at age 13—and that's considered late from a junior golf standpoint). The summer months are the best time to for a player to practice the fundamentals since the golf swing does take time to master (and there are exceptions to the rule, i.e., if one is very athletic from the start), patience may wear thin if one fails to see immediate improvement. Corporate folks or anyone starting the game past their teenage years would be at a disadvantage because of their practice time is hampered by career and family. Back when I started it was the unwritten rule to start the game as early as possible of this reason. However, there are outliers. From a golf historical note, three-time major champion Larry Nelson started playing golf in his early twenties. Bottom line, it's never too late to start!

Swing Hard in Case You Hit It

Tom Stevens

WARDROBE AND EQUIPMENT

Dress for Success

I know, I know, wearing bright colors does make you stand out in the crowd, but wearing loose-fitting clothes i.e., pants or slacks (or a dress/shorts) is just as important. Here's a breakdown of the fabrics[2]:

	Advantages	Disadvantages
Cotton	Soft. Great for sensitive skin. Warm in cold weather.	Fades quickly over time. Tough to swing.
Polyester	Lighter than cotton. Dries faster. More flexible. Easier to swing.	Holds odor longer.

---

[2] http://www.abceurope.org/different-types-of-fabrics-for-golf-shirts/

Since you're in a working environment, try to pick an outfit that's not too revealing (i.e., no tight dresses, denim, beach wear, swim wear, and not wearing underwear). In terms of hats, I recommend hats from Mission[3]—this is not an endorsement but I've had great success with this product in very hot temperatures, because it helps cool my head and is a good sweat trapper (review the great deals on Amazon, where shirt prices range from $11.00 to $75.00). Some of the pricier clothing are located in stores such as Dicks Sporting Goods, Golf Galaxy, or Edwin Watts. Why start off on a bad foot, especially if this is a corporate function; get yourself some proper gear. If you're a frequent participant at any golf course or driving range, I'm sure the pro shop will offer you a deal.

Equipment (US dollars)

Clubs

By far, my favorite portion of the book! At this point in your golf development, just visit a golf shop which has a simulator or driving range with rental clubs, and hit balls (more on that later). However, don't get me wrong, while the lofts are important in terms of distance, at this point of learning, it's not what I would focus on. Nevertheless, there are plenty of websites denoting the lie/lofts of each club[4].

---

[3] www.mission.com

[4] https://www.golfbidder.co.uk/golf-advice/519/golf-club-loft-and-lie-buyers-guide.html

Swing Hard in Case You Hit It

There are no good or bad club manufacturers. I'm sure you've heard of these companies: Ben Hogan, Titleist, Mizuno, Wilson, Nike, Calloway, Ping, Ram, Srixon, TaylorMade, etc.

Since you're a beginner, I believe it's economically wise to purchase a starter's set; you can find these at any golf shop or departmental stores. The reason I say this is that golf is a sport that requires a plurality of equipment: shoes, clubs, balls, bags, hats, shirts and pants. It's daunting to the wallet at first, depending on your locale and income.

In terms of costs, the price of clubs today has increased significantly over the past 40 years. I purchased my third set of clubs, the Hogan Apex II, 3-PW for $350.00 in 1986. Reviewing a very old October 1982 Golf Digest, the back of the magazine had a list of prices from the Las Vegas Discount Golf, where the Wilson Staff Tour was priced at $189.99, and the 3-PW with the TopFlight XL driver was $54.00.[5]

Today, an average set of irons i.e., 3-PW, costs approximately $900.00 to $1300.00, with a TaylorMade M3 driver selling for $500.00. For the novice golfer, these are the price points. When I started, my father purchased me a driver, 3, 5, 7, and a pitching wedge for, I am guessing, in 1978 prices, approximately $78.00. To save some money, visit golf outlets such as Golf Galaxy

---

[5] Golf Digest, October 1982.

or Edwin Watts that have used golf clubs, or venture online at www.3balls.com. This on-line site, for example, has, as the time of me writing this book, a used set of TaylorMade M2, 2017 version between $382.00 and $620.00. However, a better deal (as of May 9, 2018), can be found at Kmart where 3-metal woods, 6-irons, a putter, and a golf bag were priced at $129.00![6] While taking your lessons, ask the teaching professional what is best, given your level of development. Heck I still play a two-piece ball (Srixon Soft Feel White) since I want to get as much distance as I can (yes, I know spin rate can be an issue; more on that later).

Just like with club manufacturers, there's no "great shoe" that will turn your handicap from a 40 to a 5!! Any golf outlet or high-end sporting goods store will have the latest and greatest in soft spike golf shoes: Foot Joy aka "Dry Joys", Adidas, Under Amour, Nike, Skechers, etc. Try out a variety that's comfortable for your feet as well as your wallet.

<u>Balls</u>

For balls, golf balls that is, go for the cheapest ones at this point. I have nothing against the Titleist Pro V1s, but paying over $30.00 at this point in your learning curve is unwise. By all means, we live in a free society, with the exception of North Korea, but right now, the

---

[6] http://www.kmart.com/intech-magnum-men-s-golf-combo/p-080W003346768000P?plpSellerId=Kmart&prdNo=3&blockNo=3&blockType=G3

basics of the swing are alien to your body and mistakes are evident; thus, balls will be lost.

The cost benefit to buying high end over $40.00 balls would be a deficit for you, so take the pressure off yourself and purchase discounted balls. On the technical side, you may hear all the time on golf telecasts and commercials about these different layers of balls (e.g., 1-piece, 2-piece, etc.). Golf Digest stated it best by saying the following:

> *"The one common piece on all balls is the cover. Each item beneath the cover counts as an additional piece. The most complex golf balls contain five pieces, including a core, plus three separate, inner layers.* [7]

---

[7] https://golftips.golfweek.usatoday.com/inside-golf-ball-20206.html

General Golf Ball Properties Per Skill Level (As of October 2021)		
2-Piece	3-Piece	4 and 5-Piece
For Average Players.	For advanced players.	For professionals typically.
For Long Distance.	Some forgiveness.	Reacts better to different swing speeds.
Less Spin.	More spin.	More spin.

In terms of cost, in general, the 2-piece Srixon is $30, 3-pieces are a little over $30, the 4-piece Titleist can be as high as $50, and the 5-piece TaylorMade TP5, for example, is $50.

Swing Hard in Case You Hit It

Example of Current Golf Ball Manufacturers (As of October 2021)			
2-Piece	3-Piece	4-Piece	5-Piece
Calloway Warbird	Titleist Pro V1	Titleist Pro V1 x	TaylorMade TP5
Srixon Hi-Spin	TaylorMade Project	Calloway 2018 Chrome	TaylorMade TP5 x
Dunlop Lo Co	Bridgestone Tour BX	Srizon Z-Star XV	
	Maxfli Tour X		

Each set of layers have their own special features, which you can find from Golf Info Guide[8] as well as the Golf Storage Guide.[9]

As an outlier, the Maxfli Tour X is interesting. This is a 4-piece ball at the 2-piece price of $35.00! Now that's a steal.[10]

---

[8] https://golf-info-guide.com/golf-tips/equipment-choices/golf-ball-layers/

[9] https://www.golfstorageguide.com

[10] https://www.dickssportinggoods.com/p/maxfli-2019-tour-x-matte-white-golf-balls-19maxmmxfltrxmttwgbl/19maxmmxfltrxmttwgbl

Tom Stevens

Swing Hard in Case You Hit It

Lately, on tour, you hear a great deal of information regarding ball spin rates. Let's quickly dive into this. Graff Golf explains it in details:

"Every golf ball has somewhere in the neighborhood of 300-500 dimples with most balls being in the high 300's. The dimples are there to help lift the ball by forcing airflow downwards so the ball can be pushed upwards. This is a process that sends the ball spinning backwards after impact, at thousands of revolutions per minute.

The amount of spin in this process, which is called spin rate, is a major influencer of height and distance in a golf shot. With all other variables being equal, there are two primary factors that increase spin rate:

More loft. A 7-iron would have more spin than a 5-iron, for example. A good analogy here is a tennis racket. If you wanted to hit a high-arching shot where the tennis ball hits the court and stops, you sky instead of pointing it perpendicular to the ground. The same principle is true in golf. The more the clubface is pointed up to you, the more spin you are likely going to apply. This is assuming all other factors in your swing stay the same.

More clubhead speed. A stronger, faster player hitting a 9-iron will generally produce more spin than someone who hits the same 9-iron but swings slower. If you flipped a coin without much force, it may only go end-over-end a few times. With more energy, it can go end-over-end dozens of times.

Let's start with a simple example. When the average PGA Tour player hits a driver, their spin rate is typically in the area of 2,700 RPMs. For a player who is a scratch handicap, their average is right around 2,900 RPMs. If you are a 10-handicap, you are probably around 3,200 RPMs.

Of course, the better players are swinging faster, but they are typically using less loft and stiffer shafts to produce a lower launch. They also have a shallower angle of attack into the ball and make contact higher on the clubface. All of that combines to make for less spin and longer carry distances."[11]

Now, taking this into consideration, range balls are a different story. Mygolfspy.com recently wrote a story about why range balls should never be used when getting fitted for new clubs because the range of ball spin rates are dramatically different. One funny but important point was, "...you don't play with a range ball, so why use one when getting fitted..."

Here's what the guys at My Golf Spy found out, and the results were fascinating.

"Let's start with the driver. Across the three swing speeds we tested (85, 100 and 115 mph), the range balls spun about 250 rpm more than the average ball in our test. To put this in context, 250 rpm is in the ballpark of what we'd expect to see from adding a degree of loft. Effectively, the range balls we tested would make a 9.5-degree driver spin like a 10.5. With irons, the spin differences are bigger still. I'd classify them as massive.

---

[11] https://graff.golf/spin-rate-in-golf-how-you-can-interpret-your-golf-balls-spin.

For the slowest speed we tested, the range balls produced about 600 rpm more spin off an 8-iron than the average ball (and a Pro V1), and 1,200 rpm more than the lowest-spinning ball we tested (Bridgestone Tour B RX)."

My Golf Spy's Range Ball Test (Slow Swing Speed) 8-iron Speed Backspin Rates (rpm)	
Pinnacle Range Ball	7080
Titleist Pro V1	6015
Difference	1065

Range Ball Test (Mid Swing Speed) 8-iron Speed Backspin Rates (rpm)	
Pinnacle Range Ball	7080
Titleist Pro V1	5968
Difference	1112

In summary, regardless of swing speed in this instance, the range ball spin rates are significantly higher than regular commercial golf balls, thus influencing the shot distances.

For slow-swing speed golfers, range balls reached peak heights 5-yards closer to the hitting area. For mid- swing-speed players, it was 3-yards and for high swing speed players more than 10 over the average ball (and approximately 7-yards sooner than the latest peaking).

	Peak Height/Cary Distance 8-iron Mid Swing (yards)
Pinnacle Range Ball (Average)	27/158.9
Titleist Pro V1	24.7/154.7

"Percentage wise, it's an appreciable though not massive difference, but it's one more thing that illustrates the differences between range balls and the balls you (hopefully) play."[12]

This empirical evidence is an eye opener! I knew range balls produced inflated distance results, such that the rule I heard from a few golf teaching pros was to add 10

---

[12] https://mygolfspy.com/7-reasons-why-range-balls-shouldnt-be-a-part-of-your-next-fitting/

percent to the distance indicated on the rangefinder after each hit, which makes sense now, because the higher spin rates reduce distance, therefore adding the said 10 percent brings it close to the actual distance.

Golf Bags

Golf bags, in general, come in four types—carry, push cart, tour bags and Sunday bags. Carry bags are typically less than 10-lbs with approximately 7 to 10 pockets with 3 to 5 club dividers.

Push cart bags are typically bulkier than carry bags with more club dividers. Tour bags are what you see on television, usually weighing approximately 13-lbs with the same number of pockets as the carry bag, made by the major golf equipment manufacturers. I know they look heavy, but the materials used are lighter for long haul walking.

The Sunday bag or "pencil bags", as I call them, are for a few clubs one wants to work on, let's say, chipping, without dragging the whole set. There are too many bags to document. Most, if not all, major golf equipment manufacturers have at least a carry bag and a tour bag.[13] Golf Support has noted a simple summary of the different bags; however, take a look at the Titleist golf bags to get a general idea of the types of bags available.[14]

---

[13] https://golfsupport.com/blog/different-types-of-golf-bag-explained/

[14] https://www.titleist.com/golf-gear/golf-bags/

Since I'm a Ben Hogan fan, I have a few of the carry bags.[15]

Scorecard Holders

The pros on television have these fancy scorecard holders with lots of paper involving the scorecard, pin sheets, local rule notes, etc. If you walk, these are a must have. There are many options such as the Seamus, Tin Box Partners, Bluegrass Fairway, Sun Fish Golf, and Buck Magnussen. I have two Magnussons, each of them in portrait configuration.

---

[15] https://benhogangolf.com/collections/golf-bags

Swing Hard in Case You Hit It

2021 Golf Card Holders (US dollars)				
Manufacture	Pros	Cons	Size	Cost
Seamus[16]	Buchanan Field Book	Orange Leather	4" x 6.5" Folded	$95.00
Tin Box Leather[17]	Captain America	White Leather	N/A	$125.00
Sun Fish Sales[18]	Thin Blue Line Flag	Hand-Stitched Leather	7 1/2" x 4 1/2"	$44.99
Buck Magnussen[19]	Rustic Interior	Hand-made leather	4.5" x 6.5"	$185.00

Seamus is very exotic looking, with the UK plaid. By the looks of it, it doesn't seem water resistant and can over time destroy it. Box Leather emphasizes embroidering catch phrases, while Sun Fish has the most options by way of flags, catch phrases, social symbols, and even John Daly's Lion logo. Buck Magnussen is of stylish leather with stitched-edged embroidery, with the option

---

[16] https://www.seamusgolf.com/collections/scorecard-holder/products/buchanan-field-book

[17] https://www.tinboxpartners.com/store.html

[18] https://www.sunfishsales.com/product/thin-blue-line-flag-scorecard-yardage-book-holder/

[19] https://buckmagnussen.com/product/custom-scorecard-cover-rustic-leather-st-andrews/

of placing any alphanumeric lettering one wants. Since they use full grain leather, it explains the above average cost. They even have two versions—one where it opens from the top to bottom and another from left to right. However, be careful of the leather models in heat, they hold sweat in the worst way. I've also found a set of scorecard holders from Golfers Authority, but most of the materials and designs are similar. Moreover, all of it appears to be about style rather than the strength of materials in my opinion, but take a look for yourself.[20]

Gloves

Why do we wear gloves? From my research, it is to avoid injury and to prevent the club from turning in the player's hand by providing more friction and resisting moisture in humid and wet weather. In terms of injuries, it helps prevent calluses on the hand and fingers that may occur because the material texture of the grip is rough.[21] Another reason, as superficial as it, is that it looks cool—probably the second most interesting subject of my research for this book. Alex Morgan's article, "Why Do Golfers Wear Gloves? The Full Story," states that when Arnold Palmer, Jack Nicklaus and Gary Player were on tour in the 1960s, when golf became very popular, folks noticed these players wearing gloves—thus, gloves became the cool look. The article also

---

[20] https://golfersauthority.com/best-scorecard-holders/

[21] http://golftips.golfweek.com/purpose-golf-glove-1543.html

provides a technical explanation as to why one glove is used:

> *"Because when a player grips the club, the top hand is the leading hand. It's the hand that maintains full contact the entire time with the grip of the club, while the bottom hand only partly grasps the grip because it's also grasping part of the lead hand. If a player were to wear the glove on their dominate hand and that hand was to perspire, then the player could lose grip causing the club to slip, and the swing to suffer."* [22]

Huh?? This is too much information for me. I'll go along with the blister avoidance and the cool look. Again, it's another situation where you must visit a golf shop and try various types and sizes, **or** don't wear one at all—it's all up to you!

Regarding costs, the average cost of most gloves, regardless of manufacture, is approximately $22 to 26. In the following table again is My Golf Spy's glove testing synopsis.

---

[22] Alex Morgan, "Why Do Golfers Wear Gloves? The Full Story." https://www.glovesmag.com/golfers-wear-gloves/

Swing Hard in Case You Hit It

2020 Golf Glove Ratings (US dollars)				
Manufacture	Pros	Cons	Other	Cost
Mizuno Elite	Mesh material placement allows breathability and flexibility.	Velcro lacks durability.	The placement of the mesh material across the knuckles is part of a winning design with construction dedicated to flexibility and grip.	$15.99 (Amazon)
Ping Sport	Breathable and comfortable.	Material slightly thicker than others.	Built like a premium glove, the Sport provides a relaxed fit at pressure points, though it might be tight on your thumb and forefinger.	$14.99 (Global Golf)
Titleist Players Fit	Good flexibility.	Tight Fit.	It's easy to stay connected to the club. The Flex features soft leather which allows it to live up to its name.	$21.99 (Amazon)
Ping Sport Tech	Breathable.	Material is thick and stiff.	A quality performance glove, but not up to the same standards as the Sport. The Sport Tech is comfortable and is well constructed.	$14.99 (Global Golf)
Srixon All Weather	True size to fit.	Material in fingers too loose.	All Weather has a great grip and it doesn't twist during a swing. It's a reliable, comfortable glove for a bargain price.	$9.99 (Amazon)

Tom Stevens

Swing Hard in Case You Hit It

<u>Range/Distance Finders</u>

Digital rangefinders were a new golf gadget I was apprehensive of when they first came into prominence. Several years ago, I played at the University of South Florida (USF) and looked in the pro shop for a yardage book. I asked one of the players on the USF women's golf team if her course had yardage books and was f flabbergasted when she stated, "We don't have yardage books here." That's when I finally relinquished the tradition of feeling for distance and purchased a Bushnell Tour V4 (with slope factor).

You often hear about and see all these range trackers, be it at your local range or on golf telecasts, and I find them very helpful. If you have just purchased a set of clubs (new or used), it's going to take an especially long time to get acclimated to the characteristics of your sticks. There are several on the market, and most of them are not cheap: Swing Caddy, Trackman, Arccos Caddy, Ernest Sports.

The Ernest Sports ES-14 comes with a tracking device and a phone app that records your data via Bluetooth. What I do next is email the data for each club session to my email account and migrate it to an Excel sheet where each line lists the club with two columns: average distance and longest distance. Then, I condense all the data to a large-sized credit card, print, and laminate it—and it fits perfectly in my Buck Magnussen scorecard holder.

Swing Hard in Case You Hit It

Tom Stevens

Swing Hard in Case You Hit It

*Club	Average(yards)	Max(yards)
Driver	282	306
3_metal	249	284
20 (4)	214	235
24 (5)	202	221
28 (6)	192	216
32 (7)	170	178
36 (8)	160	168
40 (9)	142	156
44(PW)	131	141
44 (PW) 0.5	122	128
50	109	117
54	96	105
60/62	80	99

*These are my Ben Hogan PTx Irons. Clubs are indicated by lofts next to their equivalent traditional club number; distances are measured in yards.

Tom Stevens

Swing Hard in Case You Hit It

Below are samples of My Golf Spy's testing and analysis and distance tracking devices for the ranges.

\	\	\	\	\
2020 Golf Rangefinder Ratings (US dollars)				
Manufacture	Pros	Cons	Other	Cost
Bushnell Pro XE	Quickly acquires and locks on to target.	Red yardage display can fade in and out.	This rangefinder also considers your climate. It accounts for altitude as well as temperatures.	$549.99 (PGA Tour Superstore)
Nikon Cool Shot Pro Stabilized	Accurate yardage readouts.	Device is small.	When you've found your target, a large green circle appears, which is similar to a visual jolt.	$449.99 (PGA Tour Superstore)
Bushnell Tour V5 Shift	Quickly acquires and locks on to targets.	Doesn't account for temperature and altitude in yardage calculation.	Does calculate slope for increased accuracy. It also gives both a visual and jolt notification when you've locked onto your target.	$540.10 (Amazon)
Bushnell Tour V5	Quickly acquires and locks on to targets.	Doesn't calculate for slope or climate conditions in yardage read out.	It's the third-tier option but a great choice for those who want a Bushnell rangefinder without all the bells and whistles.	$299.99 (PGA Tour Superstore)
Precision Pro NX7	Vibration alert when target. is locked.	There are faster models on the market.	It vibrates when you've acquired your target. for added assurance.	$199.99 (Amazon)

Tom Stevens

Swing Hard in Case You Hit It

2021 Launch Monitors (US dollars)				
Manufacture	Nomenclature	Wireless/Mobile App	Size	Cost
Swing Caddy[23]	SC 200	No/No	N/A	$349.99
Trackman[24]	Trackman 4	Yes/Yes	11.8 x 11.8 x 1.8 in	e-mail for price
Arccos[25]	Arccos Caddy	Yes/Yes	Software downloads to phone.	Various monthly plans.
Ernest Sports[26]	ES-14	Yes/Yes	N/A	$400.00

---

[23] https://voicecaddie.com/products/practice/swing-caddie/swing-caddie-sc200-plus/

[24] https://www.trackman.com/golf/simulator/tech-specs

[25] https://www.arccosgolf.com/pages/rangefinder

[26] https://www.ernestsports.com

HEALTH

Rest

Since you're new to the game, put your best foot forward by not being intoxicated. We've all been at a place where it takes you 9 holes to get warmed up. Whether you're playing with a superior, subordinate(s), colleague or other people who work for and/or with you, it's not a great look. It's best not to drink alcohol in these situations. Don't get me wrong, one drink is not going to get you fired, but the last thing you want is to have upper management gazing at you, taking mental notes on your alcohol consumption that may be used against you in the next evaluation.

Additionally, find a meal that you won't gorge on, such that it has you running to the bathroom several times during the round. Now from experience that devouring nachos with various pieces of meat, jalapenos, and onions, then washing it down with several **containers** of beer, then playing a full 18 holes the next morning is NOT A GOOD IDEA! Why is this significant? Well, because I've done it! Do you really want to be the source of "morning breeze" in your group? Not exactly, it isn't a great start prior to heading to the first tee—the one reason I've never been enthusiastic about morning tee times.

But, if one is interested in nutrition based on blood types, take a look at a book called *Eat Right for Your Type* by Dr. Peter J. D'Adamo and Catherine Whitney.[27] This book covers the list of the five major food groups for each blood type as well as a history of each blood type, based on human migrations throughout the centuries (including alcohol, yes, you heard right!). You can read it while you're on the toilet disposing of the nachos you had the night before.

Without straying too far off topic, D'Adamo's book revealed that people with type A+ blood stress on vegetables i.e., they are mostly vegetarians! Ouch! But I still love my steaks. Be that as it may, it answers the questions of why during some rounds I felt bloated! So, why not take heed of your food and alcohol consumption the night before a round of golf. Don't forget that you're new to the game, so why not "blend in" with the others in your group. Wake up with a fresh and clear head, ready for conversation and action!

Stretching/Practice Before the Round

This applies to us older folks, but also to players in their 20–40s—stretching! Nothing is more frustrating than pulling a muscle before or during a round. Now, I'm not a nutritionist or a sports therapist—nor am I pretending to be one— but I always stretch my back, calves, and lower arms. In particular, I've found another article on the Internet that covers all the muscles that need to be stretched.[28] Here's a summary:

---

[27] D'Adamo, Dr. Peter J., Eat Right For Your Type. New York: Berkley Books.1996.

[28] https://www.healthline.com/health/9-stretches-to-benefit-your-golf-game#loosen-your-back

Swing Hard in Case You Hit It

Stretching Your Hips (Thighs and Back)

1. Start by facing the back of a bench/chair, with your feet shoulder-width apart. Hold the back of the bench/chair and take a step back until your arms are extended.
2. Lower your upper body, keeping your back straight. Continue until you feel a stretch in your armpits. Hold for 30 seconds.
3. Repeat 2 to 5 times on each side.

Stretching Your Hips 2 (Thighs and Back)

1. Sit up straight on a bench/chair/the floor. Put your left ankle on top of your right thigh. Plant your right foot on the ground.
2. Move your torso forward, bending at your waist. Continue until you feel a stretch in your left hip. Hold for 30 seconds.
3. Repeat 2 to 5 times on each side.

Stretching Your Elbows

1. Extend your right arm in front of you. Face your palm down.
2. Use your left hand to pull your right fingers down and toward your body. Hold for 30 seconds.
3. Return your palm to the starting position. With your left hand, pull your wrist up and toward your body. Hold for 30 seconds. This completes one rep.

Swing Hard in Case You Hit It

Complete 2 to 5 reps for each side.

Stretching Your Wrists

1. Press your palms together. Place them in front of your chest.
2. Move your hands toward your waist keeping your palms flat against each other.
3. Hold for 30 seconds. Repeat 2 to 5 times.

Stretching Your Core (Stomach Muscles)

1. Stand up straight, with your feet shoulder- width apart. Cross your arms over your chest.
2. Bend your knees and lean your upper body slightly forward.
3. Turn your torso to mimic your backswing. Pause.
4. Rotate your body to mimic your follow-through. Hold for 30 seconds.

Repeat 2 to 5 times.

Stretching Your Hamstrings

1. Place your golf club behind your shoulders, holding one end in each hand. Stand in front of a step.
2. Set your right heel on top of the step, knee bent slightly. Lean forward at your waist, with your back straight.
3. Rotate your upper body to the right. Hold for 30 seconds. Repeat to the left. This completes one rep.

4. Switch legs and repeat. Complete 2 to 5 reps for each side.

Stretching Your Shoulders

1. Start with your feet shoulder-width apart. Raise your right arm across your chest, placing the opposite hand on your right elbow.
2. Move your right wrist toward your left, pointing your thumb upward.
3. Rotate your torso to the left, tugging on your right elbow. Hold for 30 seconds.
4. Now switch hands and hold your left elbow with your right hand. Turn your torso to the right and hold for 30 seconds.

Repeat 2 to 5 times.

Eating/Drinking During the Round

Since we've covered eating and drinking before the round, let's talk about food and liquids during the round.

Find a beverage/food that's not going to cause sleep deprivation and/or gas. The last thing you want to do is expel gas on someone's backswing, yes, I've seen it done before! Reminiscing a bit, decades ago, while I was in the military, a senior master sergeant with a few other staff sergeants and myself were playing a course in upstate New York, and he really let it rip—the gas right on his own back swing (loud too)—and he hit the ball dead straight. Meanwhile, the rest of us busted a gut laughing. One guy nearly fell into the bunker near the teeing ground, and I nearly fell on the tee marker! Never got to ask him if he'd eaten the nachos the previous night—oh well.

Notably, alcohol, particularly on very hot days, dehydrates your body and decreases your concentration. In the past, I've seen guys practically pass out drinking a case of beer in 100-degree heat. One or two is not going to kill you, but I would suggest waiting till you get to the 19th hole.

Hygiene

Mouthwash or chewing gum is imperative to personal hygiene, and everyone appreciates it. However, it's best not to wear cologne because it can draw insects depending on the course, especially mosquitoes on courses such as wastelands and ponds. Therefore, insect repellant is a better choice.

An incident comes to mind of a time when I used to work at a golf course's backshop as a kid. Early in the mornings, precisely at 6 am on Saturday mornings, my job was to unlock the bolt connecting the steel chain to the golf carts, get my copy of the starter's sheet, load the golf bags onto the carts, wipe the dew off the seats, and then drive them down to the first hole. The golfers would then arrive here from the parking lot. Sometimes, their hair would be wet from their morning shower, and they would be carrying a lit cigarette—Craven A (Canadian), to be exact. Brut or Old Spice (might as well stick in Hai Karate or any late 1960s/early 1970s cheap aftershave that reeks of sweat and drywall) cologne in the air, they wiped off the excess dew that had collected on the golf cart seat, ready to play. This will be you in a few years, trust me. Just recently, I played with a man and noticed he'd had a "accident" in his pants, and I did my level best to put on a good face and ignore the situation. ***Maybe he had the nachos the night before, yeesh!***

In view of the events described above, you wouldn't want to be remembered for a negative hygiene aspect, would you? Not only is it embarrassing, but it's improper. After your round, take a good hot/cold shower if showers are available.

If there aren't any, bring a change of clothes with washrags, towels, and body wash as well as flip flops/shower shoes. You'll feel refreshed and relaxed and won't have to worry about getting strange looks from those around you!

SOCIALIZING

Conversation

Let's talk about socializing during the round. *Buy a round,* but remember to keep the alcohol to a minimum. Offer a beverage "at the turn," which means the half waypoint in the round after nine holes, or flag down the cart person (why they are always women, I have no idea... well, I might have some idea).

If you're playing golf during the regular season of the PGA/LPGA tours, talk about tournaments if you can, it shows your interest in the game (e.g., as of writing this piece, Phil Mickelson's hitting of the ball while it was moving on Shinnecock's 13th hole at the U.S. Open is creating much conversation around the world). Look up your favorite golfer to see if they attended your alma mater, for example; that should generate your continued interest in the game. The reason I bring up drinking is that supervisors and management pay attention to one's drinking habits. If even one person from upper management is staring you from a distance—stop drinking alcohol immediately! It's never a good look at all, and trust me, it's a look some people never forget.

On the positive side, start with your playing partners, talk about the round, the hole positions, the grass, the weather, etc. Follow the men and/or women on tour (find out who's hot or not), you'll find plenty of resources on the Internet.[29] This will keep you in the loop of friends, proving you have, at a minimum, a general interest in the game and not just work. Demonstrating your basic knowledge of the game will raise eyebrows and concurrence from your contemporaries, further proof of your interest in the game.

After playing the first four holes is probably the best time to start talking about work. When I was in the service (US Air Force, E-2/E-3 at the time), playing with a full bird Colonel, at the starting of the 4th hole, we briefly talked about the squadron business. But I kept it general—pardon the pun—because I could feel the conversation leaning towards information gathering on certain members of the squadron (I wasn't about to be a stoolie for anyone). Looking back, (while I'm of African descent and left-handed---an anomaly in and of itself), I believe the Colonel appreciated my candor, because the reason we played together was to relax, and that we were enjoying each other's company.

Television commentators, when it comes to course conditions, are always talking about grasses. The four known types that come up in conversation are usually the following: Bermuda, Bent, Zoysia, Rye and Poa annua. Here are the basics of each grass, as stated in golftec.com, Zoysia Farm, golfwee.com and usgolftv.com, respectively.

---

[29] www.pgatour.com; www.lpga.com; http://www.espn.com/golf/; http://bleacherreport.com/golf; http://www.usga.org

- Bermuda grass is typically grainer; grows in hot climates.[30]
- Zoysia grass is a hardy grass, very thick, like walking a soft carpet; also grows in hot climates.[31]
- Bentgrass are thin dense blades of grass; tolerant to cold.[32]
- Ryegrass has a clumped fine texture; found in cool summer regions and used to overseed Bermuda.[33]
- Poa annua is a type of bluegrass with many different strains and high root densities.[34]

Now I'm sure you've heard the word aeration—the process of drilling holes into the ground and/or the green to allow air into the roots to improve soil mixture. The clumped compressed soil resembles a cork like configuration[35], where the holes are filled with topdressing. Depending on the location, courses do these processes two to three times a year; now, it can be a nuisance on the putting green but grin and bear it, for it must be done, or just wait a few weeks till the grass grows back to its original condition.

---

[30] https://www.golftec.com/blog/2016/01/golf-tips-101-playing-golf-bermuda-vs-bent-greens/

[31] http://www1.zoysiafarms.com/whzoysia.jsp

[32] https://www.thoughtco.com/what-is-bentgrass-on-golf-courses-1560765

[33] http://golftips.golfweek.com/different-kinds-grass-golf-courses-2057.html

[34] https://usgolftv.com/courses/poa-annua-grass-what-is-it-and-why-is-it-used/

[35] Wittevee, Gordon et al., Practical Golf Course Maintenance. The Magic of Greenkeeping. Hoboken, New Jersey: John Wiley & Sons, Inc.,2005.

Now some would scoff and dismiss this information as trivia, invoking the child-like response of "whatever" crap. However, if this is not within your interests, you at least now have a general idea what these grasses are while watching a golf telecast.

Humor

I recommend a book by Randy Voorhees, titled, *You Might be a Golf Nut If...* [36] If you remember to tell a few of his jokes, you'll be remembered in a positive way. One joke I had heard is, "if you can't swing a club without farting, then you're not an athlete."

Here's a few comical catch phrases I've heard over the years:

- "Laying up with a driver."
- "The poor man's Pro V1."
- "Don't use the golf cleat device to clean your teeth."
- "Don't lick your golf balls—you don't know where it's been."
- "Really, do you need to fudge your score—which is over a 100."
- "And yes, the foot wedge counts for the maximum club number of 14!!!"
- "Using the ball washer as a sexual metaphor is so wrong."

---

[36] Voorhees, Randy. You Might Be a Golf Nut If...Kansas City: Star Books,2000.

Swing Hard in Case You Hit It

- Why do you always look for your ball 10-30 yards farther than it really is?
- Why do you *attempt* hit your driver off the deck when you always hit your 3-iron much further?
- You're still in the teaching mode when you use the fairway dew as an alignment stick.
- Cart girl: Sir, why are you constantly looking at my dress? Perverted golf guy: You know the new rules about leaving the pin in, don't you?
- Company Representative: I'll give a special deal on golf balls i.e., 12 dozen at half the price.
  Assistant Pro: Why the special deal now? Company Representative: You have a member-guest tournament coming up and I know your superintendent double cuts the greens—correct?
- I don't believe Jim Nantz, Nick Faldo, and Michell Wie will come to your bachelor party's golf tournament—you can't afford them!!
- You're too passionate a golfer if you receive a cease-and-desist order from golf companies.

A few golf books I've read in my spare time:

- *The Secret of Golf…The Story of Tom Watson and Jack Nicklaus*, by Joe Posnanski: A great book about their relationships with their fathers and their college golf career.

Tom Stevens

- *Q School Confidential…Inside Golf's Cruelest Tournament* by David Gould: Great stories about the PGA tour Q-school created in 1965. Many stories of the emotional grind of earning a PGA tour card.
- *The Future of Golf…How Golf Lost its Way and How to Get it Back* by Geoff Shackleford: Covers problems with maintaining interest in the game and how to get it back.
- *Learning Golf with Manuel* by John Hayes: The 2006 World Golf Teachers Hall of Fame inductee, Manuel de la Torres, discloses his methods of teaching golf to students.
- *Uneven Lies: The Heroic Story of African-American in Golf* by Peter McDaniel and Tiger Woods: Great story of Black Americans forming their own professional golf tour, the United Golf Association, and how these men had affected the changing policies within the PGA of America.
- *You Might be a Golf Nut If…* by Randy Voohers: One of the best golf joke books out there.

I'm biased towards *Ben Hogan's Five Lessons,* written by Herbert Warren Wind, the world-renowned golf writer who came up with the phrase "Amen Corner" i.e., the three holes,11, 12, 13 at the back nine, at the Augusta National Golf Club where the Master's Tournament is held every year.[37]

This book does a great job of explaining the basics of golf. Everyone in the golf industry has heard of this book. If you want to review before purchasing it, go to the public library and check it out; you'll be glad you did!

Another is, *The Timeless Swing* by Tom Watson with Nick Seitz.[38] I prefer this book as well because, for one, I've been fascinated with Tom Watson's balance and his accuracy off the teeing ground. In my opinion, up until Sergio Garcia came on tour, Tom was the best driver on the PGA Tour. If you purchase it through Apple's iBooks, you'll find there are instructional videos added—a great bonus feature!

As I have stated before, I'm not qualified to give any advice on swing fundamentals or physical conditioning, I can only cite sources coupled with my opinion. I found this article, "Breathe Your Way to Better Posture,"[39] that I found interesting in terms of releasing stress as well as proper breathing procedures.

Giving advice while playing

I know some folks love swinging advice during a round. If you already have, and should have, a quality Class A PGA teaching professional helping you, politely decline the "involuntary advice" by saying, "Thank you, but I

---

[37] https://en.wikipedia.org/wiki/Herbert_Warren_Wind

[38] Tom Watson with Nick Seitz, The Timeless Swing, New York: Simon & Schuster, Inc.,2001.

[39] www.golf.com/instruction/breathe-your-way-better-posture

have a swing coach, and I would appreciate it if you let me apply what I've learned." Too many people I u*sed* to know clung to every word in articles from golf magazines or the Internet and then twisted it—to the detriment of the player. And thus, this leads to some folks not taking such a rejection too well. Many of the folks I've met over the years can't even follow their own advice; how stupid is that?!

THE GAME ITSELF

Plan Ahead

If possible, play the course before the outing/tournament. If you want to really impress your playing partners, take notes on the holes. Sometimes, a golf course will have yardage books—buy them! Suppose someone in your group forgets to pick one up. If that's the case, **you'll be able to provide information to the group and be recognized for being proactive**. This practice of annotating course information was invented by two-time US Amateur and Californian Gene Andrews in the 1950s, as he would pace the course to know the exact yardages for each hole. The great Jack Nicklaus heard of this idea and used it throughout his playing career.[40] YouTube even has several videos on how to read a yardage book and the pros of using one. This can be a great learning opportunity for you as well as a souvenir!

Lessons

Now, I know what you're thinking, "Lessons are hard and time-consuming, and all the time needed to practice... I just don't have it." Well, friends, that's part of the price of success. Just think back to all the time and energy you spent to become an asset to your company

---

[40] Posnanski, Joe. *The Secret of Golf*. New York: Simon, 2015.

through formal education, military experience, and/or a combination thereof. Golf is no different.

I started taking a series of lessons (I believe it was 10 lessons for less than $100) at the YMCA when I was 13. We were hitting off door mats—no joke! Well, the alternative was hitting off of thick-waxed gym floors, which the owner of the establishment would not have appreciated. Anyway, the lessons consisted mainly of the basics: the grip, stance, and follow through. The teacher said I had a natural swing. Let's face it, if you have played hockey, baseball, or tennis, the hip rotation is similar to a golf swing. But that's all I can say about that since I'm not a U.S. certified Class A teaching professional, and to avoid errors and inaccuracies, I'll end my point here. Ensure you converse with your local PGA professional for further details. After the lessons were done, I remember my dad's enthusiasm for my progress. He was so excited that he signed me up for a membership at a private golf club. I started off as a 40 handicap, and then, within three years, I was down to a 21. Within four years, I broke 80, shooting a 78!

Aside from books and interactive videos on the Internet, the local PGA teaching professional is highly recommended! The bad news is that it's going to take time and patience to get where you want to be. Until then, if you can, practice on the grass. Mats are okay (however, they'll damage your clubs over time[41] but

---

[41] https://projectgolfau.com/do-golf-mats-damage-clubs/

hitting out of the grass and viewing your divot (the hole created by the club after impact with the ball) gives you direct feedback on the trajectory of the ball. If possible, find a municipal par-3 course, aka munis—these are the best places to not only learn the basics but also to take the pressure off yourself. I believe munis are essential to maintaining interest in beginners; that is if munis stick around.

Over the past several decades, par-3 courses have been sold to residential/commercial developers. In my opinion, these munis are the only place for beginners. My reasoning behind this is the following situation I noticed on a standard 18-hole course many years ago. A foursome was taking too long to play on the first hole. It was clear that they were beginners, and one person was teaching the other three players the basics (i.e., grip and how to follow through—I couldn't believe I was watching this) because it took them more than 20 minutes to play the first hole. I questioned the marshal as to why the group on the tee couldn't be played through; his response was that they should experience playing this course (well, at an $80-weekday rate, I guess they could). While an asset to the golf course bottom line in the short term, such managerial behavior turns into a liability for the experienced player in the long term. All this does is fuel slow play to a pace where no one wants to play, and thus no one wins.

But please don't let this issue deter your golf development; however, there should be tiers of golf courses based on handicaps. After all, Bethpage Black states, home of the 2002 and 2009 U.S. Open,

"WARNING". The Black Course is an extremely difficult course which we recommend only for highly skilled golfers." Now, I have no idea how or if Bethpage enforces this policy.[42] The "I should be able to play any public golf course, regardless of my game" notion is valid from a civil rights point of view, but if the player can't break 100, how are they going to perform on a more difficult track, such as the Bethpage? Then, the beginner may say, "But I'm curious… I want to at least hit a shot where the pros played at the U.S. Open." Okay, I'll give you that; however, this leads us right back to the issue of playing time. I definitely do not plan on playing a 5+ hour round; I don't care if it's Augusta National, I'm not going to do it.

So again, it's back to the big bucks, aka, the bottom line. Corporate management or the city/county council, whoever owns Bethpage, must reach their milestones every year, and more players mean more revenue—it's that simple. However, the slow play situation appears again, causing a domino effect: if the rounds are played by high handicap players, the time per round increases, i.e., 5+ hour rounds, thus decreasing or even phasing out the experienced players. This causes a drop in golf course revenue and dilutes the course's positive reputation!

Therefore, I hope organizations such as the USGA, First Tee program, and PGAs of the world take heed of this

---

[42] https://www.golfdigest.com/story/warning-bethpage-black

issue. Now, I'm sure I'm not the first to raise these points, but at least these organizations can gain from my perspective. So, I firmly believe that there should be a tiered golf course system for players of every skill level by way of handicap, which can at least directly address the slow play situation.

Rules of Golf[43]

I know the rules are daunting and confusing at times. Still, every institution has set guidelines, and golf is no exception. The following are basics every golfer should know, or if not, know where to look. The etiquette section of the rule book, for example, covers the following: looking for a lost ball for no longer than 5 minutes and replacing ball marks on the greens. If the ball is in the bunker, after playing your shot, rake your ball and footprints, so it's clean for others. Replace your divots to maintain the course conditions. After all, you'd be annoyed if your ball landed into a divot or unraked bunker.

Water hazards are any form of sea, lake, pond, river, and are marked with yellow states/paint. The margins extend vertically upward and downwards. On the other hand, lateral water hazards (marked with red stakes/paint) have the same characteristics as general water hazards but are deemed by course managers as an I impractical place to drop the ball. With the water hazard is the option to place the ball back into play. Now, here's an important

---

[43] United States Golf Association, Rules of Golf, 33rd Edition, effective January 2016.

distinction that is not emphasized on television—the differences between yellow stakes/paint, red stakes/paint, and white stakes/paint. With the assistance of Ms. Daniela Lendl from the USGA, here's a breakdown of the differences:

When your ball comes to rest in a water hazard (yellow), you have two one-stroke penalty options. However, when your ball comes to rest in a lateral water hazard (red), you have three one-stroke penalty options. Review the highlighted procedures for each hazard below.

If a player's ball comes to rest in a water hazard (yellow stakes), the player may play the ball as it lies in there, without penalty or under the penalty of one stroke, proceeding with one of the following options (a or b) under Rule 26-1 (Water Hazards):

a. Proceed under the stroke and distance provision of Rule 27-1 (Lost Ball or Out of Bounds; Provisional Ball) by playing a ball as nearly as possible to the spot from which the original ball was last played (see Rule 20-5, Abnormal Ground Conditions, Imbedded Ball and Wrong Putting Green).

b. Drop a ball behind the water hazard, keeping the point, at which, the original ball last crossed the margin of the water hazard directly between the hole and the spot on which the ball is dropped, with no limit on how far behind the water hazard the ball may be dropped.

Please note that if the player proceeds under Rule 26-1b (Water Hazards), the ball must be dropped behind the water hazard—see Decision 26-1/1.5 (The meaning of "Behind" in Rule 26-1).

If a player's ball comes to rest in a lateral water hazard (i.e., red stakes), the player may play the ball as it lies in the lateral water hazard, without penalty or under the penalty of one stroke, proceeding with one of the following options (a, b, or c) under Rule 26-1 (Water Hazards):

    a. Proceed under the stroke and distance provision of Rule 27-1 (Stroke and Distance; Ball Out of Bounds; Ball Not Found Within Five Minutes) by playing a ball as nearly as possible to the spot from which the original ball was last played (see Rule 20-5, Making the Next Stroke from Where Previous Stroke Made).

    b. Drop a ball behind the water hazard, keeping the point at which, the original ball last crossed the margin of the water hazard directly between the hole and the spot on which the ball was dropped, with no limit on how far behind the water hazard the ball may be dropped.

    c. As additional options are available only if the ball last crosses the margin of a lateral water hazard, drop a ball outside the water hazard within two club-lengths of and not nearer the hole than (i) the point where the original ball last crossed the margin of the water hazard or (ii) a point on the opposite margin of the water hazard equidistant from the hole.

Please refer to Decision 26-1/15 (Procedure for Relief from Lateral Water Hazard) for an illustration of the procedures for relief from a lateral water hazard.

As far as club lengths go, how many does one get? The Florida State Golf Association's website simplifies the following guidelines from the Rules of Golf[44]:

1. If you are taking <u>free relief</u>, you may be:
    a. Dropping *within one club-length* of a reference point (i.e., cart path relief), or
    b. Dropping *as near as possible* to a spot (i.e., relief for an embedded ball), not within one club-length, or
    c. Placing *at the nearest spot* that avoids interference (i.e., casual water relief on the putting green), once again not within one club-length.
2. If you are paying the golf gods a <u>penalty stroke in taking relief</u>, you may be:
    a. Dropping *within two club-lengths* of a reference point (i.e., third option of an unplayable ball or a lateral water hazard), or
    b. Dropping *as near as possible to an imaginary line,* keeping a reference point between

---

[44] https://www.fsga.org/sections/content/eRevision---Rules---120114/554

you and the flagstick and going back as far as you want (i.e., second option of an unplayable ball or second option of the water hazard rule).
c. Playing another ball *from where you last played* (stroke and distance), and it will depend from which part of the course you last played on how to proceed, as follows:
d. From the teeing ground—it may be played from anywhere within the teeing ground, from the surface of the ground or from a tee.
e. From through the green or a hazard—it must be dropped.
f. From the putting green—it must be placed.

In short, you have 1-club length for free relief (e.g., man-made objects) and 2-club lengths for relief in view of a penalty (e.g., water hazards or out of bounds fence).

White stakes/paint and walls, fences, and railings are used to indicate the boundary of the course (see the definition for out of bounds). For example, if you hit a ball past the white stake, you must play your next short from the previous spot (see Rule 20-6). *Note*: If your ball goes into a homeowner's yard—do not trespass; just leave it. I've seen irate homeowners approach golfers trespassing on their property. Forget about it and focus on the next shot (this is why you purchase the cheap golf balls).

Swing Hard in Case You Hit It

Here's an interesting take on giving advice during the round. Whenever I watch a golf tournament live, signs are posted to not speak (i.e., volunteer advise) to the players during the round. Well, here's the definition and rule that covers it:

Advice

Any verbal comment or action (such as showing what club was just used to make a (*stroke*) that is intended to influence a player in:

- Choosing a club,
- Making a *stroke*, or
- Deciding how to play during a hole or *round*.

But *advice* does not include public information, such as:

- The location of things on the *course* such as the *hole*, the *putting green*, the fairway, *penalty areas*, *bunkers*, or another player's ball, or
- The distance from one point to another, or
- The Rules.

Rule 10.2(a),(b)

Tom Stevens

Swing Hard in Case You Hit It

a. Advice

During a *round*, a player must not:

- Give *advice* to anyone in the competition who is playing on the *course*,

- **Ask anyone for *advice***, other than the player's *caddie*, or

  - Touch another player's *equipment* to learn information that would be *advice* if given by or asked of the other player (such as touching the other player's clubs or bag to see what club is being used).

This does not apply before a *round*, while play is stopped under Rule 5.7a or between *rounds* in a competition.

See Rules 22, 23 and 24 (in forms of play involving *partners*, a player may give *advice* to his or her *partner* or the partner's *caddie* and may ask the *partner* or partners' caddie for advice.

b. Other Help

(1) **Pointing Out Line of Play for Ball Anywhere Except on Putting Green**. A player may have his or her line of play pointed out by:

Tom Stevens

- Having his or her caddie or any other person stand on or close to the player's line of play to show where it is, **but** that person must move away before the stroke is made.

- Having an object (such as a bag or towel) set down on the course to show the line of play, but the object must be removed before the stroke is made.

(2) **Pointing Out Line of Play for Ball on Putting Green**. Before the stroke is made, only the player and his or her caddie may point out the player's line of play **but** with these limitations:

- The player or caddie may touch the putting green with a hand, foot or anything he or she is holding, **but** must not improve the conditions affecting the stroke in breach of Rule 8.1a, and

- The player or caddie must not set an object down anywhere on or off the putting green to show the line of play. This is not allowed even if that object is removed before the stroke is made.

While the stroke is being made, the caddie must not deliberately stand in a location on or close to the player's line of play or do anything else (such as pointing out a spot on the putting green) to point out the line of play.

Exception—Caddie Attending Flagstick:

The caddie may stand in a location on or close to the player's line of play to attend the flagstick.

(3) **No Setting Down Object to Help in Taking Stance**. A player must not take a stance for the stroke using any object that was set down by or for the player to help in lining up his or her feet or body, such as a club set down on the ground to show the line of play.

If the player takes a stance in breach of this Rule, he or she cannot avoid penalty by backing away from the stance and removing the object.

(4) **Restriction on Caddie Standing Behind Player**. When a player begins taking a stance for the stroke and until the stroke is made:

- The player's caddie must not deliberately stand in a location on or close to an extension of the line of play behind the ball for any reason.

- If the player takes a stance in breach of this Rule, he or she cannot avoid penalty by backing away.

Exception—Ball on Putting Green: When the player's ball is on the putting green, there is no penalty under this Rule if the player backs away from the stance and does not begin to take the stance again until after the caddie has moved out of that location.

If you like to test your newfound knowledge, visit the USGA website for the rule quiz.[45] The quiz is divided into three sections (basic, advanced, and a random- mix basic and advanced) with each section having 10, 18, and 25 questions, respectively, and the choice to make it an interactive (taking the quiz on the computer) session or print out a copy. I found it to be a great learning tool to clear up confusion as well as memorize some wacky definitions, e.g., rub in the green, which means a ball has been accidentally deflected or stopped by an outside agency—not literally rubbing the green (which sounds like a joke, right?). Here, the outside agency is anything under the sun that causes your ball to move when at rest or stops moving it when in motion. This involves dogs, ants, goffers, the CIA, RCMP, Contras, Backstreet Boys, the "you the man" guy, and of course, the "get in the hole" guy, among others—you get the idea!

But, all humor aside, take the quizzes! Starting with the basics, take 10 questions at a time; that's what I did. If I was able to understand one section of rules, I also read it and marked it with a highlighter and/or annotated the rule in the blank pages at the back of the rule book.

---

[45] https://www.usga.org/rulesquiz/rules_quizzes.html

Note: To become a USGA member and get the rules of golf book for free, all you have to pay for is shipping and handling.[46]

---

[46] http://www.usga.org/content/usga/home-page/clubhouse/default/2017/members-join.html

PUTTING IT ALL TOGETHER

During the Round

If you're within the last 4 holes of the round, why not challenge yourself. Here are some examples: try to one putt three of the last four holes; get at least two drives on the fairway; hit at least one green in regulation; blast a sand shot within a foot of the hole (if applicable). Any one of these scenarios would be great not only for you but to leave a lasting impression on your game companions.

When you're just beginning the game, there's nothing more frustrating than not hitting the shot you have planned. But do your level best to keep the swearing down, and by any means, don't throw clubs! One story comes to mind. A former playing partner (not mentioned in the dedication, by the way) hit his shot—which wasn't all that bad—but was so frustrated with his attempt that he threw his club high toward one of the trees on the hole we were playing, and it got stuck in the branches. Naturally, he was embarrassed that he had to get the green staff to get the club out of the tree.

It happens to the best of us, where nothing seems to be working during the round, but it's always that one shot that has you cheering for yourself. For instance, I once had one of those disastrous rounds where I couldn't hit a fairway even if my life depended on it. Then, as soon as I hit the 18th hole, I made a 50- foot putt! ***Unfortunately,***

it was for a bogey. It's just one of those things that happen; all I can say is, that's golf.

To quote the great Ben Hogan, "As you walk down the fairway of life, you must smell the roses, for you only get to play one round." His point is that just enjoy the environment! The problem most golfers have (which applies to me whole-heartedly) is rumination. According to many psychologists and mental health professionals, rumination is defined as the human mind restating a negative event or series of events repeatedly for a certain duration. The solution is mindfulness, which forces the mind to stay in the present, to cease ruminating about the bad shots in previous holes.

To add, pay attention to the course conditions: wind direction, slope of the land, air conditions (ball travels farther in humid and hot conditions; ball smaller distances in cold air). It is extremely frustrating to hit an approach shot short of the green because of the wind howling into your face or because you did not realize the sand was so firm that the bounce on your wedge fails to skip the sand; instead, you blade it 50 yards over the green. These factors are the beginning of your training in course management.

Lastly, take a group picture as well as a few pictures of the course, especially of a hole you were proficient on, as a keepsake of the one or plurality of great shots, and remember to post it on social media. You can even challenge one of your playing partners to match play (see USGA rule book rule 2 for the basics). This could be an opportunity to show off your skills to your boss. First of all, the old adage of "letting your boss win" is a joke. Tanking a round shows little class, which raises the question of your ethics. After all, your behavior on the course translates into what the management thinks of you in the capacity of your job.

Another incident I'll never forget is when I played a couple of rounds with my squadron commander's boss—a Full Bird Colonel. Months passed, and my section supervisor told me that I was not allowed to play with the Colonel because there was some work that needed to be done, but the Colonel insisted that we play on that specific day. That afternoon, my section supervisor walked into the room, tail between his legs, telling me that I'd be playing with the Colonel at 4:30 pm. All the while, I kept thinking, **"Yeah, no shit, sir!"** The Colonel was impressed with my game and how I carried myself on the course, so much so that we became very good friends until his retirement. In this instance, it was our love for the game where rank had no privilege—*well, sort of!*

I remember another incident from about six years later when I was an engineering technician under a defense contractor, and I played a company tournament with the CEO. I barely knew him, but we had hit it off. I just banked on my experiences playing with the Colonel, and that was all. A few days later, my supervisor at the time picked up the phone with his eyes agape to say that the CEO wanted to speak to me (I didn't have my own phone number yet, I'd been with the company only a few months) to let me know he couldn't make it—this simple call blew my supervisor's mind! It also led to many outings with him and upper management.

Most memorable was his private company tournament with our senior-level military personnel and other league tournaments at the U.S. Naval Academy. Speaking of the Naval Academy, at the time, while our firm had access to the course, Head Pro and Navy Golf Coach Pat Owen thought I was a student until I told him otherwise. To this day, his assumption is very flattering. Although I left Maryland in 2014, we're still good friends.

In summary, the game brings people together, regardless of company title or military rank. For this lesson in socialization, I have to thank my Dad because of what he taught me indirectly—golf is a great social outlet in business and in life. So, don't quit the game. There are plenty of local area golf courses providing lessons. And here's some more advice: don't get mad at the teacher if they are solving a problem with your swing. Chances are there's an underlining problem that's the source of your issue.

For example, years ago, I was trying to get rid of a torrid hook. I couldn't fix it on my own, so I got a 15-minute lesson from a pro at a golf show. I explained the problem, he had me hit a few balls, and then he delved into the grip. Internally, I was agitated at him for not directly addressing my hook problem, which I thought was due to a bad swing plane. Turns out he was explaining and correcting my bad grip, which was the underlining cause of the bad hook (Boy, that was a lesson in and of itself).

You may wonder why a teacher sometimes won't correct the other swing flaws during your session; it is because they want you to focus on one issue at a time. And so, it's not a money s squeeze, as you may think. The swing is a complex set of integral moving parts such as grip, stance, posture, weight transfer, weight position on certain shots, arm position, hand position on the club, and swing plane, just to name a few. To fix a plurality of problems in a session is impossible. Therefore, take a series of lessons with one teacher you are comfortable with and trust.

CONCLUSION

Another means to better your game is to watch the tournaments on television, especially the majors! Traditionally, some would argue that the tournament seasons start with the Masters (men) and the Chevron Championship (women). Even the casual sports fan watches these two tournaments. I always favored the U.S. Open because it's "Open" to anyone and for men with a handicap index of 1.4 and below. These qualifiers, the ones I've attended over the years, whether local or sectional, are always free and sometimes have a better field than a PGA tournament. A prime example of this was in the middle 1990s, during the former Kemper Open (now called the Wells Fargo Open) at the TPC Avenel in Potomac, Maryland. Sometimes, it had weak fields where few top 20 players on the money list appeared due to scheduling conflicts, but more so because of the course itself. The original course design (now revamped) was not a tour stop favorite (as per Greg Norman's highly critical remarks[47]). A week after Kemper, the U.S. Open sectional qualifying at Woodmont CC in Rockville, Maryland, had players skipping the Kemper to compete in the 36-hole qualifier. Again, this was, and perhaps still is, free. Here's a sample of the loaded field of talent in 1994 Many of these names

---

[47] https://www.washingtonpost.com/sports/golf/pga-tour-pros-hated-tpc-avenel-enter-tpc-potomac-for-the-quicken-loans-national/2017/06/28/8fbfcbf0-5c27-11e7-9b7d-14576dc0f39d_story.html

Swing Hard in Case You Hit It

I'm sure you'd heard of, either in the broadcast booth or on the senior tour:

- Robert Gamez, Bill Britton, Lenny Clemens
- Wayne Levi, Rodger Maltbie, Guy Boros
- Kenny Perry, Bob Burns, Donny Hammond
- Bill Glasson, Vince Heafner, Joel Edwards
- Andrew Magee, Stan Utley, Doug Martin
- David Toms, Lanny Wadkins, Billy Ray Brown
- Tommy Amour III, Justin Leonard, Jay Delsing
- Keith Clearwater, Grant Waite, Brad Faxon
- Kelly Mitchum, David Duval, Bobby Watkins
- Robert Wrenn, Neal Lancaster, David Peoples
- Duffy Waldorf, Marco Dawson, Jim Carter
- David Feherty, Mike Hulbert, Tom Byrum
- Joel Edwards, Buddy Gardner, Gary Hallberg
- Joey Sindelar, Steve Pate, Mark O'Meara

And again, these qualifiers are *free*.

Another fun option—volunteering to help manage the tournament. This encompasses assisting in the pre-setup of the tournament (marshaling), guiding patrons where to walk, registering players, and attending to parking (see the link below[48]). Here is the volunteer description from the 2022 Memorial Tournament[49]:

---

[48] https://www.pgatour.com/impact/2019/06/12/make-impact-your-community-volunteering-pga-tour-event.html

[49] https://volunteers.thememorialtournament.com/faqs/view

Swing Hard in Case You Hit It

Basic responsibilities:

- Smile and make visitors feel welcome and appreciated.
- Be attentive to your position on the grounds or at your designated location.
- Be respectful of players, sponsors, spectators, Club members, and fellow volunteers.
- Be flexible; if you are available to work additional shifts, please let your Committee Chair know.
- Report in full uniform ON TIME and READY TO WORK your shift. There could be heavy traffic; please plan accordingly.
- Check your email frequently during tournament week and the day you are volunteering. Email will be the primary means of communication for weather delays or additional coverage needed for your assigned shift.

Shifts	Benefits Received
8 Hours	• ONE set of meal coupons (1 sandwich, 1 snack, 1 non-alcoholic drink) is good only on the day(s) you are volunteering • ONE Volunteer Badge (good for admittance each day of tournament week) and ONE course entrance gate voucher for a guest (good for any one single-day admission)

Tom Stevens

Swing Hard in Case You Hit It

	• ONE parking pass to the A Lot* parking lot, good on the day(s) you are volunteering (If other parking is provided based on volunteer assignment, no parking pass will be issued.)
9–11 Hours	• TWO sets of meal coupons (1 sandwich, 1 snack, 1 non-alcoholic drink, each) are good only on the day(s) you are volunteering • ONE Volunteer Badge (good for admittance each day of tournament week) and ONE course entrance gate voucher for a guest (good for any one single-day admission) • ONE parking pass to the A Lot* parking lot, good on the day(s) you are volunteering (If other parking is provided based on volunteer assignment, no parking pass will be issued.)
12+ Hours	• TWO sets of meal coupons (1 sandwich, 1 snack, 1 non-alcoholic drink, each) are good only on the day(s) you are volunteering • ONE Volunteer Badge (for admittance each day of tournament week) and ONE Patron Badge for a guest (good for admittance each day of tournament week) • ONE parking pass to the A Lot* parking lot, good on the day(s) you are volunteering (If other parking is provided based on volunteer assignment, no parking pass will be issued.)

The number of hours/days/shifts varies depending on the volunteer area.

Tom Stevens

- The minimum number of days for the Mobile Device Courtesy Committee is 2 days.
- The minimum number of days for Marshals is 5 days: 4 Tournament days (Thursday through Sunday) and 1 practice day (Monday, Tuesday, or Wednesday)
- The minimum number of hours for all other volunteers is 8 hours.

Those exempted from these guidelines include EMS and Shuttle Drivers. View the EMS and Shuttle Driver FAQs to see the requirements for these committees.

Various volunteer assignments

- Bears
- Clubhouse Ambassadors
- Concessions
- Courtesy Cars
- Disabled Services
- Hospitality
- Leader Boards
- Will Call/VIP Courtesy Center
- Player Evacuation
- Patron Information
- Sandwich Factory
- Scoring and Data Control
- Status Boards
- Supply Distribution

- Volunteer Committee

Volunteers have to pay for their uniforms. Yes, it may sound not very advantageous, but in view of the benefits (i.e., the chance to see world-class players), some would argue it's worth it.

All general volunteers must adhere to the uniform requirements unless specifically noted under each unique committee description.

- The official uniform consists of the yellow Memorial Tournament polo shirt. The shirt must have the current logo.
- Men may wear khaki (tan) long pants and closed-toe shoes.
- Ladies may wear khaki (tan) slacks, capri pants, shorts, or skorts and closed-toe shoes. Shorts and skorts must be walking length or just above the knee.
- Hats and visors should have the current logo or no logo.
- Jackets must have the current logo or no logo.
- Remember, only uniform pieces with the current logo can be worn during volunteer shifts.

Over the years, I've had friends volunteer for the U.S. Open, Canadian Open, Kemper Open, and the Valspar Tournament in Palm Harbor, Florida. Only one person out of the group didn't appreciate the experience (the long hours bothered him). I can understand watching guys playing a great course that you can't play; I'm the same—I'd rather play. However, I would recommend you view the whole process, from the players applying a ruling to them processing their routines on the range, viewing their equipment (my favorite), as well as their swings. This was my routine, especially if I needed a new short game routine (i.e., Phill Mickelson at the 2021 Valspar).

Well that about covers it, until the next edition. Good luck with your game, and most importantly, have fun!!

Made in the USA
Monee, IL
15 April 2024

2b1cc23f-f5d6-4b96-8155-224d6d01a6a6R02